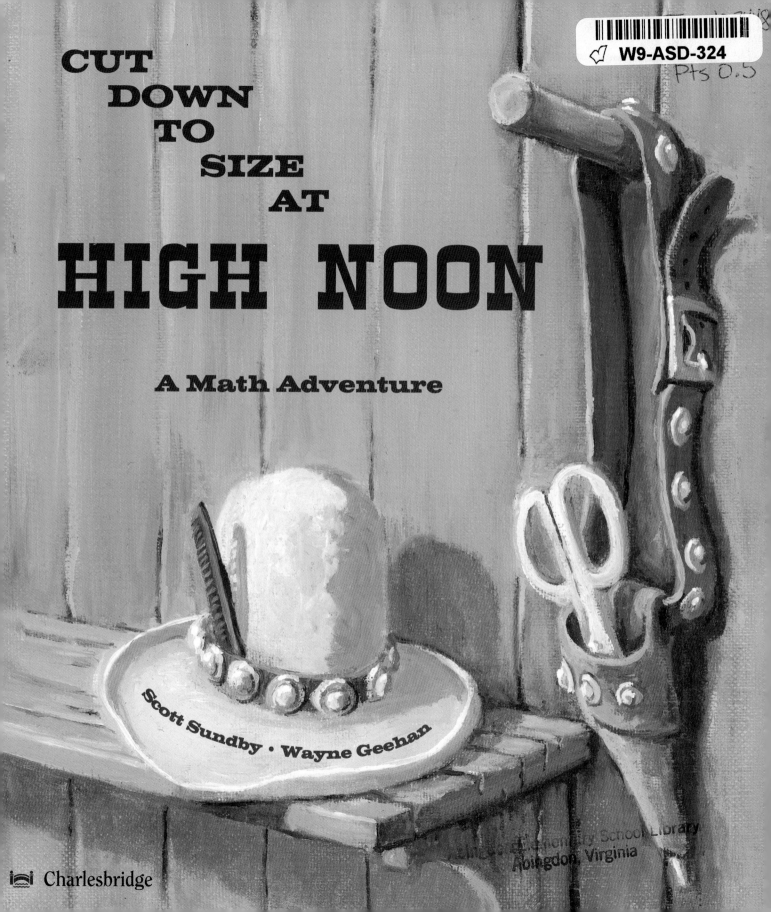

CUT DOWN TO SIZE AT HIGH NOON

A Math Adventure

Scott Sundby • Wayne Geehan

Charlesbridge

To Taylor, for trusting Dad to cut his hair, and to Katie, Christopher and Kelsey, for helping convince him that the unusual result was actually a work of art. — S.S.

For my friends, Frank Burr, Wayne McCarthy, and Walter Keyes. — W.G.

Text copyright ©2000 by Scott Sundby
Illustrations copyright ©2000 by Wayne Geehan

Published by Charlesbridge, 85 Main Street, Watertown, MA 02472
(617) 926-0329 • www.charlesbridge.com

Library of Congress Cataloging-in-Publication Data
Sundby, Scott
  Cut down to size at high noon : a math adventure / Scott Sundby ; Wayne Geehan [illustrator].
    p. cm.
  Summary: A showdown between two barbers in the frontier town of
Cowlick leads them to realize new uses for scale drawing.
  ISBN-13: 978-1-57091-168-2 (softcover)
  ISBN-10: 1-57091-168-1 (softcover)
  1. Drawing—Technique—Juvenile literature. [1. Drawing—Technique.]
I. Geehan, Wayne, ill. II. Title.
NC655 .S86 2000
813'.6—dc21   00-029444

Printed July 2010 by Sung In Printing
in Gunpo-Si, Kyonggi-Do, Korea
10 9 8 7

At first glance, Cowlick looked just like any other small frontier town. The people who lived there looked just like average, everyday folk.

That is, until their hats came off.

4

The person responsible was Louie Cutorze. Louie was originally from France. Rumor had it that he was once the haircutter to the king, but an accidental nip of a royal ear had made it necessary for Louie and his family to leave the country.

Louie's hair creations were the pride of Cowlick.

The key to Louie's fantastic haircuts was scale drawing. Louie measured a life-sized thing, then used the measurements to create an exact drawing of it, only smaller. Based on the drawing, Louie cut and sculpted and brushed and combed until — *voilà!* — you had a cow on your cranium or a hog on your noggin.

Louie's son Harry was the only one who knew how he did it.

Scale-Down Steps

1. Measure the life-sized object.
2. Decide what scale to use, such as 4 inches = 1 square.
3. Divide to reduce the parts equally.   48 inch tail
   48 ÷ 4 = 12 squares
4. Use the scale measurements to make a small scale drawing.

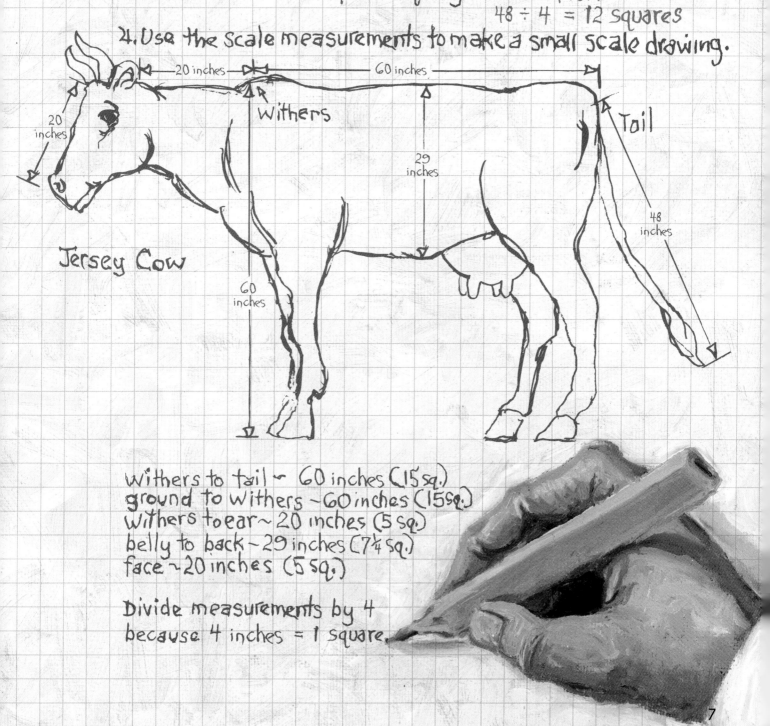

20 inches

60 inches

Withers

Tail

20 inches

29 inches

48 inches

Jersey Cow

60 inches

Withers to tail ~ 60 inches (15 sq.)
ground to withers ~ 60 inches (15 sq.)
withers to ear ~ 20 inches (5 sq.)
belly to back ~ 29 inches (7¼ sq.)
face ~ 20 inches (5 sq.)

Divide measurements by 4
because 4 inches = 1 square.

"Today," Louie told Doc Lane, "I think I will give you something especially useful."

"What's it going to be?" asked Doc.

"Just wait and see," Louie said with a mysterious smile. "I guarantee you'll like it."

Bald Eagle

84"

40"

25"

3" = 1 square

And he was right. Doc Lane was mighty pleased
with his new haircut, especially when it rained.

9

Daisy Jenkins always asked for "Just the usual, Louie." Daisy knew that you never got "the usual" when Louie cut your hair.

"But, of course!" laughed Louie good-naturedly.

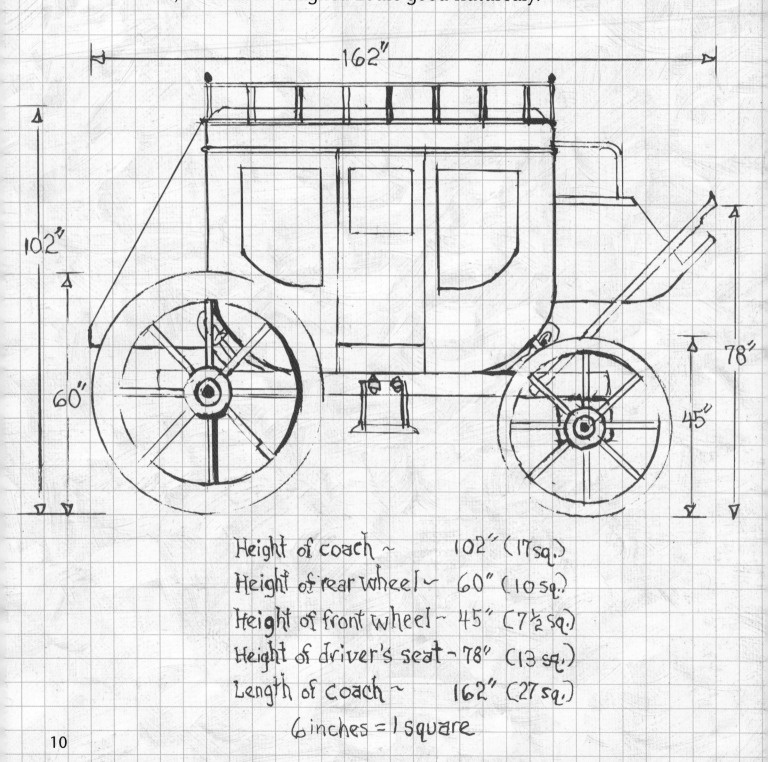

Height of coach ~ 102" (17 sq.)
Height of rear wheel ~ 60" (10 sq.)
Height of front wheel ~ 45" (7½ sq.)
Height of driver's seat ~ 78" (13 sq.)
Length of coach ~ 162" (27 sq.)
6 inches = 1 square

Daisy and her three children all got something out of the ordinary — just as she had expected.

One morning, as Louie cut and Harry swept up the
clippings, the door to the shop burst open. There stood a
stranger, all dressed in black. In a voice that sounded like gravel
beneath a boot, he said, "Name's Buzzsaw — Buzzsaw Bart. I've
heard tell of your fancy, French haircutting, and I don't like it one bit."

"I want my hair cut the way I like, and I'll tell you exactly
how to do it," Buzzsaw demanded with a sneer. Then he
let loose a challenging laugh that echoed through the
room like a midnight thunderstorm.

13

Now, no one told Louie how to cut hair.
He needed complete artistic freedom.
Depending on his mood, you might leave his shop
with a bluebird or a vulture atop your head. Louie
wasn't about to let this Buzzsaw character push him around.

14

"I've never seen you around these parts before. What brings you to Cowlick, stranger?" he asked.

"I'm here to set up shop," Buzzsaw smirked. "I'm a barber. In fact, I'm the best barber in the West."

"There's room for only one of us in this town," Louie said defiantly.

"I reckon we'll just have to see about that," Buzzsaw snarled.

"Meet me on Main Street at high noon for a showdown.
Then we'll see who sticks around and who hits the trail."

"You will,"
said Louis.

"No, you will,"
said Buzzsaw.

"I'll stay,"
said Louis.

"No, you'll
leave," said
Buzzsaw.

And with that, Buzzsaw Bart stomped out.

Louie snipped and cut until there
was a falcon battling with a snake
on Bad Luck Billy's head.

"Gosh, Louie, he's a mean one. What are
you going to do?" Bad Luck Billy asked.

"Do?" Louie laughed. "Why, I'm going to cut
that dull-edged varmint down to size!"

17

As the sun rose in the sky and high noon approached, all of Cowlick turned out onto Main Street, milling around like a bunch of restless cattle before a storm.

The rustling and whispering died down when Louie
and Buzzsaw stepped out into the middle of the
street and squinted at each other.

Then, as the sun reached
its zenith, the two men
strode toward each
other until they were
face to face, their
hands poised above
their holsters.

The town clock struck
twelve.

Faster than a rattlesnake strikes, they drew their weapons. Louie raised his scissors and started snipping and shearing furiously at Buzzsaw's hair. Buzzsaw started clipping and cropping Louie's hair with equal speed.

Although the sun that day was blazing away in a clear blue sky, so much hair started to fly that soon it was as dark as a moonless night.

The crowd tried to peer through that cloud of hair, but it was no use. They'd just have to wait for the two to finish what they had started.

And then, suddenly, the cutting stopped. Hair quietly fluttered onto the dusty street.

When the air cleared, the crowd gasped in astonishment.
The sheriff slowly stepped forward and held up two mirrors.
Buzzsaw and Louie gazed silently at their reflections as the crowd waited.

Finally, the glimmer of a smile began to tug at the corners of Louie's lips. Buzzsaw, too, started to grin. The crowd stirred in relief.

"Amazing," said Louie. "I've never before had something that is really so small fit so artfully on my head."

"And I've never had something that is so big fit so skillfully on mine," said Buzzsaw.

"What's your secret?" they asked each other at the same time.

Buzzsaw spent the rest of the day showing Louie how to use scale drawings to make small things bigger. First, Buzzsaw measured every part of a life-sized object.

Then, he multiplied the size of each part equally, until he had created an exact model of the original object on a larger scale.

Grasshopper

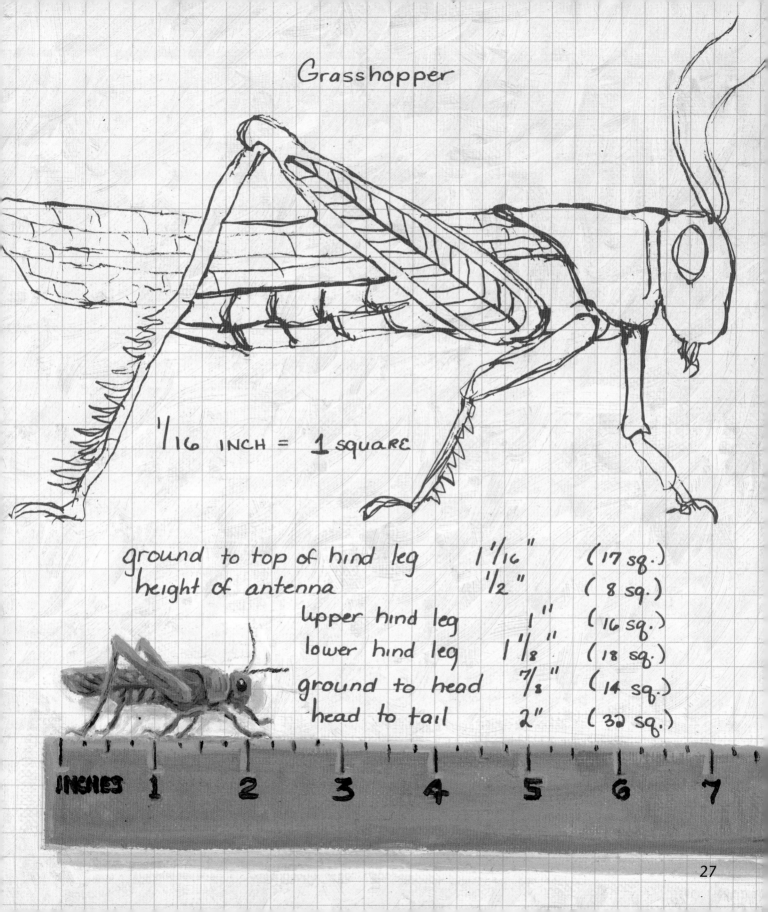

¹/₁₆ INCH = 1 SQUARE

ground to top of hind leg	1¹/₁₆"	(17 sq.)
height of antenna	¹/₂"	(8 sq.)
upper hind leg	1"	(16 sq.)
lower hind leg	1¹/₈"	(18 sq.)
ground to head	⁷/₈"	(14 sq.)
head to tail	2"	(32 sq.)

INCHES 1 2 3 4 5 6 7

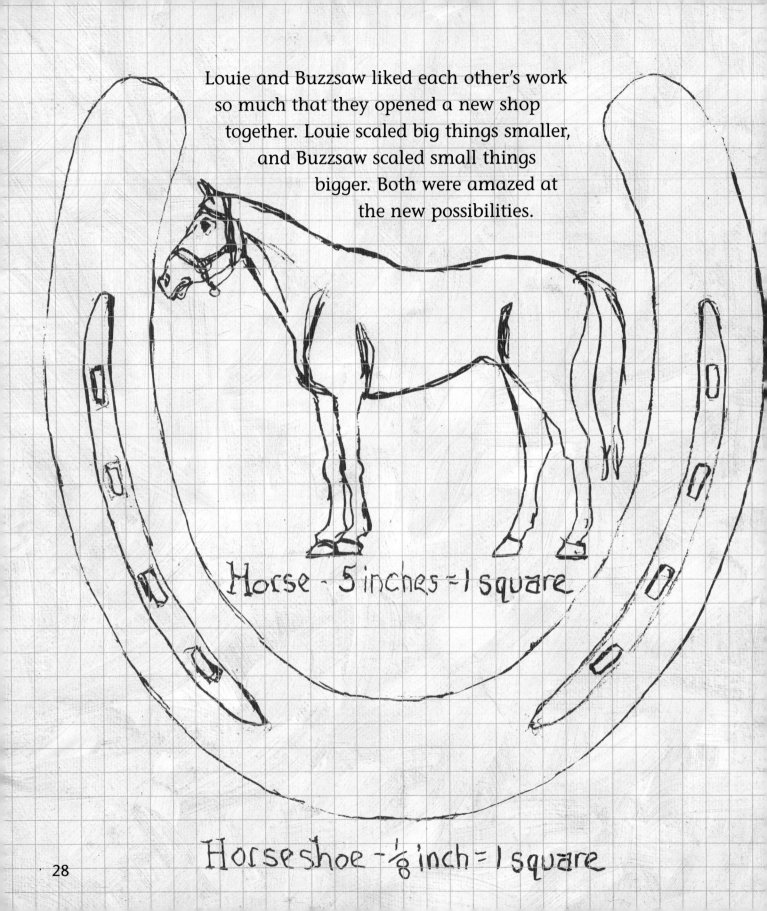

Louie and Buzzsaw liked each other's work so much that they opened a new shop together. Louie scaled big things smaller, and Buzzsaw scaled small things bigger. Both were amazed at the new possibilities.

Horse - 5 inches = 1 square

Horseshoe - 1/8 inch = 1 square

They particularly enjoyed working together.
The two of them made the town of Cowlick proud.

After their first year as business partners,
Louie and Buzzsaw had a party. They invited
the whole town and gave everybody
haircuts for free.

People came from miles around and had a hair-clipping, floor-thumping, barn-shaking good time.

And Harry found something to do with all those hair clippings.

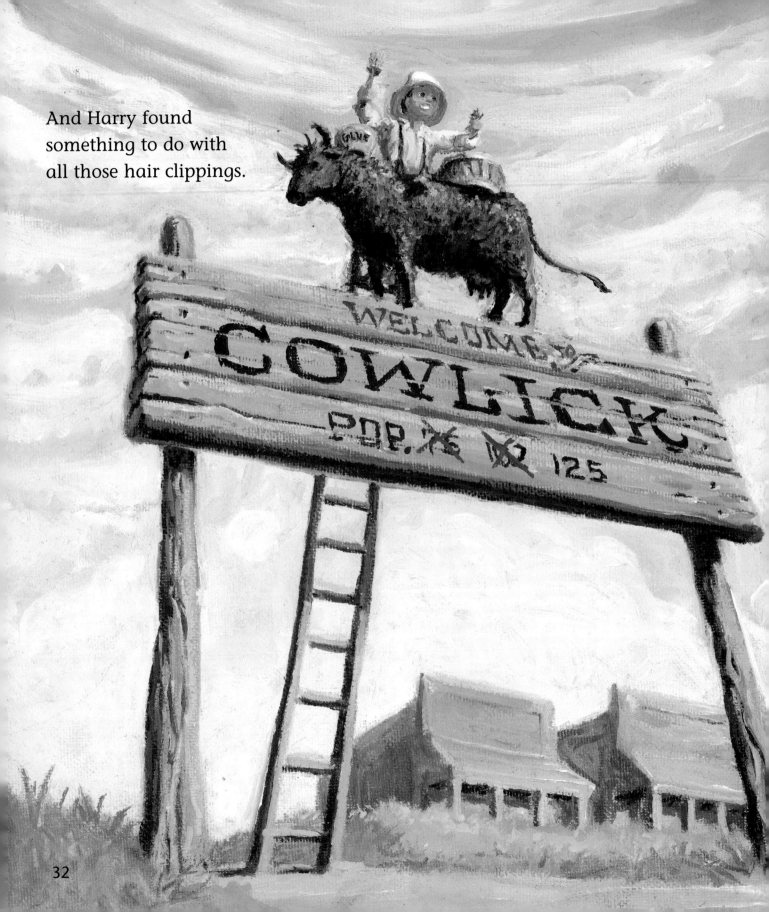

WELCOME to COWLICK

POP. 75 102 125